CLASSICAL STUDIES FOR
PICK-STYLE GUITAR

Develop Technical Proficiency with Innovative Solos and Duets

William Leavitt

Berklee Press

Director: Dave Kusek
Managing Editor: Debbie Cavalier
Marketing Manager: Ola Frank
Sr. Writer/Editor: Jonathan Feist

ISBN 978-0-634-01339-3

DISTRIBUTED BY

Berklee Press

1140 Boylston Street
Boston, MA 02215-3693 USA
(617) 747-2146

Visit Berklee Press Online at
www.berkleepress.com

HAL•LEONARD®
CORPORATION
7777 W. BLUEMOUND RD. P.O. BOX 13819
MILWAUKEE, WISCONSIN 53213

Visit Hal Leonard Online at
www.halleonard.com

Introduction

The compositions in this volume have been compiled to acquaint guitarists with some of the excellent musical literature of the past adaptable to the pick-style guitar.

With thorough study and practice, this material will definitely increase your knowledge of, and technical proficiency on, this formidable instrument.

Fingerings and positions, where indicated, are in many cases optional. (This is especially true with the Bach inventions.) Most of these passages are playable in other areas of the fingerboard, and all possibilities should eventually be sought out and practiced.

I must admit that there is still another motive in presenting this material. I sincerely hope, with the tremendous improvements that have been made in amplification of the guitar, and all of the possibilities this affords, that someday in the near future the entire musical world will recognize the pick-style guitar as a legitimate instrument of considerable stature. The skillful performance of the type of traditional music presented on the following pages cannot but help further this cause.

Table of Contents

Caprice

M. Carcassi

Allegro

M. Carcassi

(♩=120)

Waltz

M. Carcassi

6

Study In F

M. Carcassi

Etude

F. Carulli

Etude In F Major

F. Carulli

Study In C Major

F. Sor

Study In A Minor

F. Sor

Etude No. 1

Kreutzer

Etude No. 2

Kreutzer

Etude No. 3

Kreutzer

Sonatina
(Solo or Duet)

M. Clementi

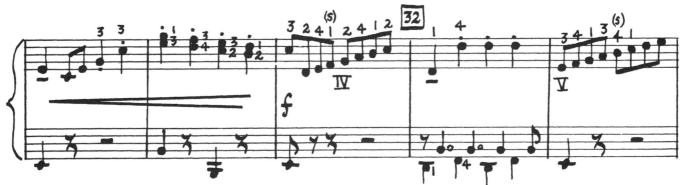

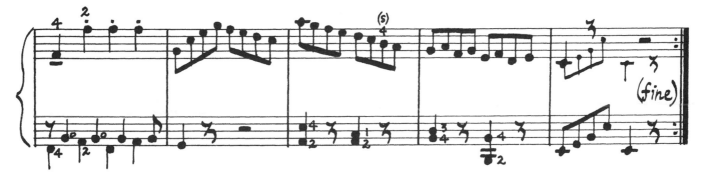

15

Invention No. 10

J.S. Bach

NOTE: IN MEASURES 20,21,22, AND 23 THE UPPER AND LOWER STAVES HAVE BEEN
SWITCHED SO AS TO MAKE A MORE COMPLETE SOLO FOR THE FIRST GUITAR.

16

Invention No. 4

J.S. Bach

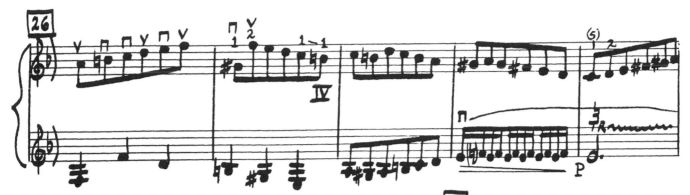

19

Invention No. 1

J.S. Bach

21

Invention No. 8

J.S. Bach

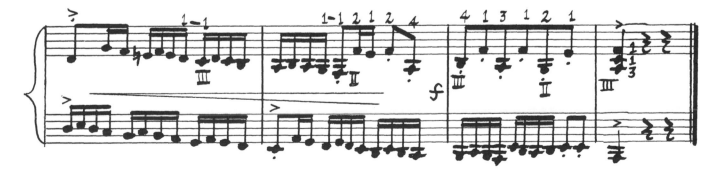

Invention No. 13

J.S. Bach

25

Invention No. 2

J.S. Bach

Excerpt From Perpetual Motion

N. Paganini

Bourree
(*from violin sonata in B minor*)

J.S. Bach

Sarabande
(*From Violin Sonata In B Minor*)   *J.S. Bach*